Coming Down
from the
Mountain:

Returning to Your Congregation

THE
EMMAUS
LIBRARY

Coming Down
from the
Mountain:
Returning to Your Congregation

Lawrence Martin

UPPER
ROOM BOOKS®
NASHVILLE

ISBN 978-0-8358-0882-8

Cover design: Jim Bateman
Seventh printing: 2007

Printed in the United States of America

Lawrence C. Martin has pastored United Methodist congregations in Ohio, Oregon, and Idaho. He is married to Linda, and together they have raised three children. Larry has participated on the Clergy Team for more than a dozen Walks. He has served on the Board of Directors for the Idaho and Oregon Trails Walk to Emmaus as well as the International Steering Committee. He is currently the pastor of Freemont United Methodist Church in Portland, Oregon.

Contents

Introduction

☩

ou have gone on the Walk to Emmaus. As you learned to say in greeting and celebration with your fellow pilgrims: *De Colores*. You remember the decorations, the singing, the feast of fellowship at each meal, the talks, and the worship of your Emmaus weekend.

If you are like me, you thought the Walk would be just another church program. You never guessed that the Walk to Emmaus would affect you so deeply. If you are typical of people who have attended the Walk, you know that through the Walk to Emmaus, God has changed your life. You were an active church member before you went on the Walk to Emmaus; and you still are, but with "a new and right spirit" within you (Psalm 51:10). You were probably a disciple of Jesus Christ before you went on the Walk to Emmaus; you tried to live your life to please God and to honor your commitment to Christ and his church. But something happened during your Walk to Emmaus that brought the gospel home to you. Maybe you understood the gospel in a deeper way because of a particular talk, or you were moved by an act of agape. Maybe you found meaning in a worship service or in knowing that people were praying for you. Whatever brought the gospel home to you—a particular experience or the whole program—you probably came away from the Walk a different person, a disciple with a renewed commitment to your faith, family, and congregation.

Renewal

The Walk to Emmaus is a unique Christian program designed to renew disciples and, through them, to renew local churches and to convert the world.

The Walk affects people deeply. Many testify that it has changed their lives; brought healing and new meaning to their minds, bodies, and spirits; and set them off on a spiritual journey that will not stop until they reach the gates of heaven. Going on the Walk to Emmaus means being intensely involved in Christian community, in and through which we are brought closer to God. We meet new friends from many denominations. We hear talks that offer an overview of basic Christian beliefs; in worship, we have a chance to approach and to be encountered by God. We listen as men and women speak the truth about themselves and passionately tell their stories of faith. We may surrender long-standing burdens and gain new insights. We may marvel at the depth of community established within our discussion groups. Though the Walk to Emmaus sounds too good to be true, anyone who has attended the Walk knows that it is an intense encounter with God and with the faith of Christ's church.

I'd like to be able to say that everyone who attends the Emmaus weekend has as good an experience as I have described. But nothing is perfect. Our plans and hopes for a particular weekend may go awry. Not every pilgrim has been blessed. But statistics and personal testimony tell us that the majority of participants have found the Walk to Emmaus an important event in their lives of Christian discipleship.

The Emmaus experience is so positive that many people find returning to their congregations problematic. That is why you are reading this booklet, and that is why I have written it.

The Walk to Emmaus is powerful, but temporary: a three-day weekend. The rest of a pilgrim's life is called the fourth day, when Emmaus participants return to their congregations. They may think of their churches as lively, spiritual homes. Or they may perceive their churches as deserts, as dry as Ezekiel's bones. Either way, Emmaus pilgrims return to their congregations to invest themselves as disciples of Jesus Christ and to bring renewal to the church.

For most of us, Emmaus is a mountaintop experience; and it is hard to come down to the valley. The mountaintop air is heady and exhilarating. The valley air is stuffy, lethargic, polluted. But we live in the valley; God leads us there to fulfill our calling as disciples.

On the Mountaintop

We are not the first to journey to the mountaintop. Read about the transfiguration in Matthew 17:1-8. Jesus took James, John, and Peter to a high mountain. While they were there, Jesus' appearance changed. "His face shone like the sun, and his clothes became dazzling white" (17:2). Suddenly, Moses and Elijah appeared on the mountain; and

Jesus stood with them. The disciples stood open-mouthed in amazement as their friend, Jesus, conversed with the great lawgiver and the prophet. The three disciples were temporarily permitted to observe the Lord in all his heavenly glory. They knew him well, but now they saw his true identity as the incarnate Son of God. And they were amazed. Never one to hesitate, Peter tried to take over: "Lord, it is good for us to be here; if you wish, I will make three dwellings here, one for you, one for Moses, and one for Elijah" (17:4). God didn't like Peter's idea. Suddenly, "a bright cloud overshadowed them" (17:5); and the voice of God came from the cloud, saying, "This is my Son, the Beloved; with him I am well pleased; listen to him!" (17:5). The disciples hit the deck in fear. The next thing they knew, Jesus was saying, "Get up and do not be afraid" (17:7). When they looked up, they saw no one but Jesus.

Matthew 17:9-20 is the rest of the story. Jesus, James, John, and Peter came down from the mountain and were met by a crowd. The other disciples had been trying to heal an epileptic boy. The boy's father told Jesus about the boy and the disciples' inability to cure him. Jesus took over, chastised the people for their lack of faith, and healed the boy. When the disciples asked why they could not cast out the demon, Jesus replied, "Because of your little faith."

The scripture portrays the ups and downs of discipleship. Discipleship includes experiences on the mountaintop and in the valleys. God graciously permits us to experience the mountaintop events. They are important, but they are also temporary and rare. As Peter found out, disciples of Christ cannot camp out on the mountaintop and forget the rest of the world. Jesus' disciples visit the mountaintop and thank God for their spiritual experiences, but they live in the valleys. And there they serve in Christ's name.

We want to prolong experiences like the Walk to Emmaus. But even if we serve as team members for another Walk, we cannot relive our first weekend. Emmaus is a once in a lifetime experience.

The Fourth Day

The beauty of the Walk to Emmaus is that it continues on the fourth day, as disciples bring renewal to their congregations. The goal of Emmaus is to make disciples, to renew congregations, and to make the world more Christian. To accomplish these goals means to come down from the mountain and to work in the valleys.

Coming down from the mountaintop of Emmaus is a necessity, a certainty, and a blessing—yes, a blessing. In the scripture, Peter, John, and James came down the mountain and joined the other disciples as they continued their journey of discipleship. The mountaintop experience was over, but it wasn't complete. There was more to learn and more to accomplish. The same is true for the Walk to Emmaus. Hundreds of thousands of Emmaus pilgrims have returned to their congregations to help God renew the church and convert the world. This booklet is dedicated to pilgrims and their sponsors, who could not have guessed what Emmaus would do for them. It is offered in the hope that when pilgrims return to their congregations, they will discover Jesus—healing, teaching, and leading his people.

The Blessed Cycle

✟

The Walk to Emmaus is an adaptation of the Roman Catholic Cursillo de Christianidad, which means little course in Christianity. Prayers and discernment for Cursillo began in 1939 by Spanish Catholic laymen who wanted to be more intentional about Christian discipleship. They designed a seventy-two-hour cloistered retreat to give people an opportunity to hear the basic doctrines of the faith, to worship, and to find a deeper sense of Christian community. During the 1960s, Protestant denominations began to offer Cursillo as a short course in Christianity. In 1978, The Upper Room began to present the Cursillo program. In 1981, The Upper Room adapted the retreat to speak more effectively to an ecumenical Protestant audience. At this time, the name of the program was changed to Walk to Emmaus. In 1984, The Upper Room developed Chrysalis, a Walk to Emmaus for youth.

God has blessed the Emmaus program. The statistics for Cursillo de Christianidad, the Walk to Emmaus, and its offspring indicate that we are not presumptuous in calling it a movement. The Walk to Emmaus alone has been a means of grace for more than half a million people in more than three hundred places, including countries such as Brazil, Australia, Mexico, Puerto Rico, Germany, Zimbabwe, and Hong Kong, as well as the United States.

I believe that God raised up people to help renew the church through Cursillo and the Walk to Emmaus. By the grace of God, the church is constantly renewing itself. The format, content, and style of the Walk to Emmaus are meeting people's deep needs for faith. The Walk has become an effective means of renewing disciples and, through them, their local congregations.

From the Church, For the Church

So Emmaus comes from the church, and it returns to the church. It is a blessed cycle. It is like the water cycle, which continues to renew the land. The rain falls, filters down to streams and rivers that lead to the ocean, and replenishes the earth. It is then drawn back into the atmosphere where the water is released again in rain. The relationship between the Walk to Emmaus and the church is a blessed cycle of renewal. The church created Emmaus, and Emmaus exists to renew the church—not the church named on a roadside bulletin board or listed in the registry of denominations, but all the churches and denominations that bring pilgrims into the Emmaus experience. The church and Emmaus live in a relationship of continuing renewal. The church, through Emmaus, quenches the pilgrims' thirst for spiritual depth; pilgrims, in turn, return to the church to help meet its needs for spiritual renewal. Each is a blessing to the other.

The church brings people to the Walk. Emmaus returns them to be intentional disciples of Jesus Christ and agents of renewal. Pilgrims return to local congregations, their primary places of discipleship, and to their homes, places of employment, and communities. Many pastors and other church leaders testify that the participants on the Walk to Emmaus return to offer themselves as selfless servants, employing their gifts and graces where they are needed in the local congregation. This is as it should be. An Australian pastor says of Emmaus, "The encouragement Emmaus gives in choosing, using, and giving people experience in being leaders is found in few other activities of the church. I have found Emmaus to be the best program for helping persons realize their leadership potential."

God's Gift

So the blessed cycle has continued for twenty years. Congregations, by way of sponsors, send disciples to the Walk to Emmaus; and Emmaus sends them back. Most have a deeper understanding of their faith and a renewed commitment to live for Jesus Christ, starting with their ministries in and through the local church. Let's not forget that the Walk to Emmaus is God's gift to the church. Emmaus does its part to encourage and empower the church's mission to "make disciples of all nations" (Matthew 28:19). God works through the efforts of all Christians and every program that builds up the faith and the church. It is important for us, as pilgrims to Emmaus, to return to our local congregations and to offer ourselves as humble servants, ready to serve the church wherever we are needed.

Long-Term Obedience in a Single Direction

✝

*Y*ou will not find the name of Friedrich Nietzsche in a list of Christian saints. He was a nineteenth-century German philosopher and atheist who had little good to say about the church or faith. He died bitter, angry, and insane. Ironically, he died in the arms of gentle nuns who took him in when the world cast him out.

Nietzsche was a brilliant analyst of history and critic of religion. He wrote, in *Beyond Good and Evil*, "What is essential 'in heaven and on earth' seems to be . . . that there should be obedience over a long period of time and in a single direction."[1]

Jesus demands long-term, consistent obedience: "No one who puts a hand to the plow and looks back is fit for the kingdom of God" (Luke 9:62). "Whoever does not carry the cross and follow me cannot be my disciple" (Luke 14:27). There was a point in Jesus' ministry when some of his disciples "turned back and no longer went about with him. So Jesus asked the twelve, 'Do you also wish to go away?' Simon Peter answered him, 'Lord, to whom can we go? You have the words of eternal life'" (John 6:66-68). It was not exactly a rousing chorus of "I'll go where you want me to go, dear Lord."[2] But the disciples realized that they were committed to Jesus for the long haul.

Christian discipleship is "obedience over a long period of time and in a single direction," under the guidance of the living Christ through the Holy Spirit. To be a disciple of Jesus Christ is to follow faithfully and obediently all the way home, uphill and down, on the mountaintops and in the valleys, with the crowd and alone.

Joy in Obedience

Following Jesus is not duty. We were created to follow Jesus, and discipleship is our hearts' desire. It is life and joy and peace and power. The church offers discipleship to everyone, knowing that acceptance brings eternal life within the serving and celebrating church on earth and in heaven. Dietrich Bonhoeffer warned against "cheap grace," the easy, ersatz discipleship prevalent in his time and in ours. He reminds us that Christianity as discipleship is both comprehensive and blessed: "Happy are they who know that discipleship simply means the life which springs from grace, and that grace simply means discipleship."[3] Grace makes Christian discipleship truly satisfying, rather than grim and duty-bound.

The Walk to Emmaus is helping the church make Christian disciples with a commitment to long-term, consistent obedience. It is doing so in a joyous, positive way and has had an impact on the church that few programs in our time have had. Emmaus is taking church members to a deeper understanding of discipleship; offering them an intimate relationship with Christ, which is their birthright as the baptized; and sending them out with renewed energy. Emmaus often revives a church member who has been a Christian for years, but has not encountered the full impact of the life-changing gospel; sometimes his or her faith has waned and weakened over the years until faith and service have become a chore. Pilgrims on the Walk discover a joy they didn't think possible and a whole new outlook on life and on the church.

The Walk to Emmaus is designed to equip disciples for "obedience over a long period of time and in a single direction." It is not designed to manipulate emotions, to give people "Jesus goose-bumps," or to provide a forum for the latest trends in theology or group dynamics. The primary purpose of the Walk to Emmaus is to motivate and prepare people for long-term obedience in the direction of Christ our Lord.

Disciples, Pilgrims, and Other Followers of Christ

Eugene Peterson, in *A Long Obedience in the Same Direction*, notes that the church has used the words *disciple* and *pilgrim* to refer to the essential identity of the Christian. The word disciple does not mean *listener, dabbler, consumer,* or *aficionado*. Peterson writes, "Disciple . . . says we are people who spend our lives apprenticed to our master, Jesus Christ. We are in a growing-learning relationship, always. A disciple is a learner, but not in the academic setting of a classroom, rather at the work site of a craftsman. We do not acquire information about God but skills in faith."[4] Likewise, when the church spoke of the Christian as a person on a faith journey, it did not use the word *tourist*. It used the word *pilgrim*. We are a people on the way to God, ultimately to heaven; but in the meantime, we are on the way to wherever we see the saving work of God in the world. A tourist meanders; a pilgrim walks with a purpose. A tourist is interested in entertainment or culture; a pilgrim is interested in truth and mission. A tourist consults a map and a guidebook; a pilgrim consults the Spirit. A tourist seeks a means of transportation; a pilgrim a means of transformation. The way of a pilgrim is Jesus Christ. The church needs more pilgrims and more disciples of Jesus Christ. God uses the Walk to Emmaus to turn some tourists into pilgrims and some consumers into disciples. Disciples realize that they are committed to long-term obedience; and by the grace of God, they welcome the challenge. If Christians take discipleship seriously, the church will be transformed and its impact on society will be staggering. The Walk to Emmaus is designed not so much to make disciples as to renew them and to renew their churches.

Sponsors or other people who talk about the purposes of Emmaus should keep in mind that Emmaus is not an evangelistic program, but a program of renewal. People who participate in the Walk are pilgrims in whom the Spirit of the Lord already dwells. Emmaus helps them to realize and accept the lordship of Christ. During the Walk, they experience the power of a Christian community that puts Christ above all other concerns, personalities, issues, and agendas. Emmaus pilgrims return to their congregations with a new vision of what the church can be under the Lordship of Jesus Christ.

Our first priority as returning pilgrims should be to keep our spiritual fires burning. Only then can we sustain "obedience over a long period of time and in a single direction." Our culture tends to value activity. We are more comfortable *doing* than *being*. Doing does not please God unless we are doing what God wants us to do, unless we are responding to God's call. Responding to God requires an ability and a willingness to pray, a certain amount of knowledge and information, and an investment of ourselves in service. (This is the three-legged stool of piety, study, and action that we heard about on our weekend Walk.)

Christiana

The Walk to Emmaus will be effective only if pilgrims tend to their souls. Christian discipleship does not depend on information, technique, or spiritual exercise. It depends on the formation of our spirits into the image of Christ so that we can witness to Christ in the church and in the world. Followers of Jesus have been called the *Christiana*, "the little Christs," because they reminded people of Jesus. One of the reasons people leave or stay away from the church is because churches bear so little resemblance to the Lord. Recently, I met a parishioner's beautiful ten-year-old granddaughter. Her name was Christiana, and I asked if she knew where her name came from and what it meant. When I told her its meaning, she beamed with joy. What would happen to congregations if they knew who they were and what their name, Christian, really meant?

Many churches are filled with burned-out clergy and laity. They have tried to do the impossible: To be Christian and to function as the church without a vital connection to Christ in piety, study, and action. Without Christ, long-term, consistent obedience is no more good news for the church than it was for Nietzsche; and the church may die bitter, angry, and insane, as he did. Learning how to love God is our best witness and our best defense against burnout and wrong turns on the journey. Loving God prepares us to hear God's call.

Emmaus is not spiritual busy-work. It should not be divisive. The church needs disciples who love God, themselves, and other people in Jesus' name and are able to speak and act from the perspective of a personal relationship with Jesus Christ. Unless pilgrims make their spiritual or devotional lives a priority, the effects of Emmaus will be short-lived, without long-term obedience or a constant direction.

Pilgrimage

Traveling together is better than traveling alone. If the people traveling together are friendly and going to the same place for the same purpose, so much the better. Christian pilgrims soon learn that it is better to travel together. Disciples learn best when they learn together. In fact, Christian discipleship requires a community. The first thing Jesus did was to establish a community, a group of disciples. He started with twelve, but the community is not complete until "every knee should bend . . . and every tongue confess that Jesus Christ is

Lord, to the glory of God the Father" (Philippians 2:10-11). We are part of the community of disciples. For most of us, the Christian community is a local congregation. The purpose of Emmaus is to help renew God's community so that disciples may travel together in the peace and power of the risen Christ. We return from Emmaus to our local congregations to extend the renewal we have received.

To Serve in Jesus' Name

We do not return to rescue the church. Christians cannot rescue themselves, much less the church. Only God can save us. We do not return to our congregations to straighten out others, to reveal a manifesto for worship or for organizational change, to persuade other people to support a social or political agenda, or to turn fellowship into a perpetual Walk to Emmaus. We return simply to love and to serve in Jesus' name (which is the purpose of congregational life). If we return humbled, we will be able to sustain our spiritual lives; and when God calls, we will be able to offer ourselves in service in our congregations. In returning from Emmaus to our congregations, we are pilgrims traveling together, with one life in Christ and with a commitment to "obedience over a long period of time and in a single direction."

Send Forth Your Spirit—
But Only to 26th and Freemont

✠

God moves in a mysterious way
His wonders to perform;
He plants His footsteps in the sea,
And rides upon the storm.

—William Cowper[5]

od is a big God with a big agenda. While God loves us deeply and is intimately concerned about us, we are not the only people on God's mind. We would be appalled if the pastor prayed on Sunday morning, "God, send forth your spirit, but only to our church, the one at Twenty-sixth and Freemont."

We assume that you have attended a Walk to Emmaus or that you are interested in Emmaus and the possibilities it holds for your life and the life of your church. But the Walk to Emmaus should be seen and understood in the context of faith: God is a big God with a big agenda for the church and the world. God blesses the Emmaus movement. God also blesses other programs, other causes, and other people. God will use any bush that will burn, and there are many bushes burning with the Spirit of God today. The Walk to Emmaus is not the only place where people are on fire for God.

Either/Or

Our culture has some problems and peculiarities, one of which is our penchant for dualism. Dualism is the assumption that reality can be neatly divided by the number two. We divide life into opposing compartments: for or against, us or them. In order to make discipleship easier, we may also think of these as opposites: sacred or secular, my people or other people, faith or works, church or world, spiritual or material. The problem with dualism is that God is not an either/or God.

Both/And

Emmaus is one program among many. It is a wonderful discipleship-renewal program that God has and will, we pray, continue to bless. But there are other programs that God will also bless. God loves the whole world; and God works out God's purpose in mysterious ways. Emmaus finds its place in the mix.

The Walk to Emmaus promotes cooperation among churches and denominations. Although it is rooted in the mission of The United Methodist Church and The Upper Room, the people involved in the Walk to Emmaus rejoice in its ecumenical nature. God uses Emmaus to bring renewal to many churches.

Roland Rink wrote in a letter about the first Walk in South Africa: "During the Soweto Walk, we had no fewer than seven different denominations. God's abiding love overarched all. There was not one word of dissent. Hymns and choruses were sung in English, Zulu, Xhosa, Sotha, and Afrikaans." Trans-denominational fellowship in the Walk to Emmaus is one of its greatest blessings.

The Church in the World

Emmaus attempts to break down the categories of church and world, sacred and secular, faith and works. One of the hopes of Emmaus is that it will bring renewal to pilgrims and, through them, to congregations. Another hope is that church members and congregations will make the world a Christian environment. Jesus said that we are the salt of the earth. Discipleship is not simply a matter of church work. God sends us out, like ambassadors or missionaries, so that we can be witnesses for God in the world.

Renewal occurs only when congregations and church members meet the world with love, service, and reconciliation. To understand discipleship as only a congregational concern is to misunderstand Christ's mission and to turn our churches into irrelevant religious ghettos. Marjorie Thompson, in *Soul Feast*, writes, "If the Word I hear Sunday morning or during my private prayer has no bearing on the way I relate to family, friend, and foe, or how I make decisions, spend my resources, and cast my vote, then my faith is fantasy."[6]

No Holiness, but Social Holiness

John Wesley thought that piety, study, and action were all important for Christian discipleship. He taught that Christians need both an inward and an outward focus and that faith has both a personal and a corporate dimension. He called Christians to be in ministry in both the church and in the world. Wesley wrote, "The gospel of Christ knows of no religion, but social; no holiness but social holiness."[7] Steve Harper says that Wesley "never believed that true devotion could ever remain individualized . . . Authentic spirituality thrusts one into mission and into the life of social holiness."[8] The Walk to Emmaus moves disciples to serve God and humanity in both the church and the world. Pilgrims return, as committed disciples, to their congregations and to the world that "God so loved" (John 3:16).

Archbishop Oscar Romero of El Salvador exemplified Christian discipleship. Romero's love of Jesus convinced him of the need to seek justice for all God's people. He thought of the church not as an institution set apart, but as a force for love and justice. Because of his ministry, he was assassinated on March 24, 1980.

May God send us into the world in the Spirit of Christ.

Aeneas or Odysseus?

✝

The Walk to Emmaus may lead people to continue their spiritual journey on new paths. Or it may bring them back to familiar settings, with renewed life and faith. The ways pilgrims return to their congregations and their daily lives depends on the directions in which the Spirit guides them. The myths of Aeneas and Odysseus tell about two men who left home to serve in the Trojan War. After the war, Aeneas traveled to Africa and then to Italy, where he finally settled. Odysseus spent ten years trying to get home and arrived with new wisdom gained from his experience. When people return from the weekend, they should try to discern where the Spirit seems to be leading them. Are they like Aeneas or Odysseus?

Tom's experience resembled Aeneas'. When he went on the Walk to Emmaus, he was a middle-aged man with a good, secure future. He had a happy marriage, a good job; and he was well-placed in church and society. The Walk caused Tom to think about his priorities and challenged some of his ideas about life and discipleship. The old patterns, comfortable as they were, no longer seemed to sustain him. Maybe they were too comfortable. The old rewards—the big house, the long vacations, the new cars—no longer delivered as much satisfaction as they had. He began to think about how he could make himself more available to God, be of more service with his time and gifts, and be a more conscientious disciple of Jesus Christ. One day, at a time when Tom was open to possibilities and perhaps more open to the Spirit, he observed a friend, a professional house painter, at work. "Do you suppose I could make a living doing that?" Tom asked. "Don't see why not," his friend replied. With the support of his wife, Tom sold his business and his big house; he started a new, less lucrative career as a house painter so that he could give more time and energy to the priorities of Christian discipleship. Tom was like Aeneas. His Walk to Emmaus led him down new paths of spiritual renewal.

Claudia was more like Odysseus. A single parent with a teenage son, Claudia sought out a church and became involved in Sunday school and youth ministry. For years before she attended the Walk to Emmaus, she faithfully served the Lord. She was a mother, an employee, and a church member; and she brought Christian faith to all aspects of her life. When a friend wanted to sponsor her for the Walk to Emmaus, she accepted. Claudia had a great time. She came back home with renewed enthusiasm and a clearer perspective on her involvement in the church. She began to see discipleship as ministry rather than duty. The Walk to Emmaus renewed her faith in Christ; she brought a new spirit to her old ministries. She said, "I was a Sunday school teacher before Emmaus, and I'm a Sunday school teacher after Emmaus." (She could have added mom, executive, committee member.) "But now I'm a better teacher because I don't have to teach; I want to."

Like Odysseus, Claudia came home with new wisdom. Claudia returned to her old life and picked up where she had left off, but she had "a new and right spirit" within her. Sometimes, when pilgrims return from the Walk to Emmaus, their eyes are opened and they see home, family, jobs, congregations in a new light, as if they were seeing them for the first time.

Called to Ministry

Some people who attend the Walk as lay people eventually become clergy. Seminary students and clergy count Emmaus among the formative factors in their call to ministry. They are like Aeneas, walking down new paths on their spiritual journey.

The Walk to Emmaus is not designed to recruit ordained ministers for the church. In fact, it is designed to give the laity a greater appreciation for their ministry. The fact that some people attend an Emmaus weekend and eventually end up in the pulpit, is perhaps a coincidence. But we believe that coincidence is actually the result of God's guidance. Certainly anyone who experiences God's call to ordained ministry should respond by following the candidacy process required by his or her denomination.

Making Changes

Some people return from Emmaus changed, and they set off in new directions. Like Aeneas, they find themselves on a spiritual journey. They should be aware of how the changes they experience affect other people. If they are surprised and maybe even frightened by the work of the Holy Spirit, imagine the feelings of their families, pastors, congregations, employers. Prayer and reflection are necessary, as is honest, humble communication. When I thought of starting a new, somewhat controversial healing ministry in my church, a veteran pastor advised, "The three rules that apply in this case are these: 1) Go slowly. 2) Go very slowly. 3) Go exceedingly slowly!" Perhaps people who find themselves looking down new paths should heed his wisdom.

Remember, when God calls people into new and different ways of life, God usually confirms the call. Like Jonah, we get the message more than once. Like Paul, we listen for confirmation by the whole church in its practices of corporate discernment. (The apostle didn't set out on his first missionary journey until the church had laid on hands and prayed.) Discerning God's will for our lives is not a simple matter, especially if we discover that God's will means a significant change, that God calls us to begin a spiritual journey or to set off on a new path.

Most of our spiritual journeys are more like odysseys. We are more likely to be the spiritual kin of Odysseus than of Aeneas. Most of us return from the Walk to Emmaus as changed people, but we do not have a radical new agenda for our lives. Instead we return to revise and refine the agenda to which God has already called us.

People like Odysseus return to where they started, but they do not come home unchanged. Every experience changes us; and important, intense, or ecstatic experiences change us even more. We cannot expect to be the same people before and after the Walk to Emmaus. Our spiritual journey is like a river that moves between the same two banks, but never stays the same.

The transition from the Emmaus weekend to the fourth day may be as important as the weekend experience itself. It is important to find out if we are like Aeneas, who set out into the world, or Odysseus, who found his way home. It is equally important to let other people know about our spiritual journeys so that they can help us return to our congregations in ways that are right for us and for the church.

Are you on like Aeneas or Odysseus?

When Your Congregation Isn't as Exciting as Emmaus

Notice that the title of this section is *"When"* — not *If*— "Your Congregation Isn't as Exciting as Emmaus." It is impossible to compare the weekend Walk with the ongoing routine of a congregation. Congregations have a wider scope of concerns and activities and have made a long-term commitment to be God's people together. Joanne Bultmeier, a layperson, points out, "One thing most pilgrims need to understand is that they can't get out of the churches what they get on their Weekends. The structure is totally different. We can't cloister members in our churches for 72 hours. Pilgrims need to realize that everything they got from their Weekend was to prepare them to return to their local churches. They should return with the attitude that 'I have been given a gift from God and I have a mission: to help, vision, work, talk, and serve in my church to help bring it along in deeper faith so it is no longer dull or boring.'"

For many people, the Walk is an invigorating, thought-provoking, life-changing experience. It is not surprising that Emmaus raises expectations of what the church can be. Pilgrims have experienced a community in which Christ is honored and brothers and sisters love one another. Some people come home all charged up, forgetting that their home churches have gone on with business as usual. The result can be a jolt for pilgrims and their churches. Pilgrims are struck by how methodical and even boring the church is. Church members who have not gone on the Walk react to Emmaus pilgrims with anxiety, appreciation, excitement, curiosity, and amazement. It is important to remember that all people express their spirituality and support the ministry of Jesus Christ in unique ways.

Pilgrims Ready to Renew the Church

Pilgrims go home ready to help renew God's church. They are not sent home to change the church into the Walk to Emmaus, to convince everyone of its merits, or to recruit more participants. The leaders of each Walk meet pilgrims where they are on their spiritual journey and invite them to grow. Pilgrims return to their churches ready to offer church members the same gracious invitation. Congregations reform at various speeds. They start at different places and travel along different routes. Congregations need love and understanding, not criticism and condemnation. Even if we return to boring congregations, we should remember that they are our boring congregations. Approaching our churches in a spirit of Christian love will help us make our churches better.

Offer Thanks

When pilgrims return from Emmaus, I remind them to thank their congregations for the opportunity of going on the Walk. Sometimes they respond, "My congregation didn't do anything." Oh yes it did! Even if you, as a pilgrim, were not sponsored by a church member, the people of your congregation nurtured you in your Christian walk and helped you become spiritually ready for the Walk to Emmaus. They helped God lay the foundation for your Emmaus experience, and they deserve thanks. In addition, many people probably helped you during the weekend. Somebody taught your Sunday school class, cared for your children, supported you in prayer. Each pilgrim's situation is different; but for everyone, congregational support helps to make the weekend possible. Returning pilgrims should say thank you. Returning with a thankful heart will calm the critical spirit that may arise from comparing congregational life with Emmaus. Even the dullest church will be improved by the pilgrim's gracious thanks.

Praise Christ

After I remind returning pilgrims to say thank you, I say, "Don't praise Emmaus as much as you praise Christ." Pilgrims and their congregations may not have Emmaus in common, but they have Christ in common. So it is important to emphasize Christ. People get tired of hearing "Emmaus, Emmaus, Emmaus." Too much talk about Emmaus fosters resentment and gives the false impression that Emmaus is the only way to renew the church. One pastor counseled, "Don't tell people what Emmaus has done for you. Tell them what Christ has done for you at the Walk to Emmaus." The Walk to Emmaus is a once in a lifetime experience. Being part of the church is a life-long vocation.

"Sell the Organ!"

Returning pilgrims and their congregations sometimes disagree about worship. During the weekend, worship is often less formal than it is in many congregations. Musical accompaniment is likely to be a guitar, rather than a pipe organ; and camp songs, rather than hymns, are more suitable for the setting. Sometimes pilgrims come back from Emmaus with a negative attitude toward more formal congregational worship: "Sell the organ. Send the hymnals to missionaries. The only valid music is Emmaus music."

Worship is important to people. Most congregations struggle to address the needs of a diverse body of people. When we return from Emmaus ready to make changes in worship, we should exercise wisdom and common sense. We should talk with our pastors, worship leaders, and committees. We should avoid talking about *us* and *them* and should not identify any music or worship as belonging solely to Emmaus. Many congregations are open to reevaluating their worship and music. Pilgrims returning from Emmaus may offer opportunities for everyone to learn about Christian worship and its vital role in the life of the church. There is room in the congregation's life for diversity. Opinions about worship need not be the occasion for strife.

Life in the Spirit

Ultimately, the Spirit gives life to a local church. If we want dull congregations to come alive, the most important thing we can do is to be open to the Spirit and to encourage others to do the same. It is amazing how exciting churches and communities become when church members begin to experience the living God. Enthusiasm is contagious. Fervent prayer has changed the atmosphere of many local churches. At Pentecost, tongues of fire rested on the heads of the disciples (Acts 2:3). The temperature of a church is raised, not by one big blast of heat, but by many little fires burning brightly together.

Many local churches testify that the Walk to Emmaus builds up the energy of the church. Worship becomes more lively and singing more spirited. People trained to give talks at Emmaus become more competent and confident leaders in the local church. Emmaus helps churches come alive. However, churches are renewed at their own pace and in a variety of ways. We must beware of expecting too much too soon. Ultimately, the Holy Spirit works through many aspects of congregational life to revive the church. We should be patient and work diligently to enliven the aspects of the church in which we are involved. God will no doubt bless our efforts.

"God's Little Dysfunctional Family"

Like families, some congregations are more mature and functional than others. Some churches suffer from major problems; some have fought for years. Some have a terminal case of boring. A pastor arrived at a new church. He was not encouraged when the departing pastor handed him the keys and said, "Welcome to God's little dysfunctional family." Sending a few people on the Walk to Emmaus will not solve all our problems or save all our churches. Not every local church will welcome returning pilgrims with open arms, and not every pastor or lay leader will be receptive to the ideas and visions of returning pilgrims. Sometimes old wineskins won't accept new wine. I pray that the Emmaus community will continue to be faithful and that God will intervene to bring health and vitality to hurting churches.

Perhaps pilgrims find themselves in difficult churches because God wants them there. Read the story of Esther. Esther was a Jew who became queen of Persia. Because of her position, she was able to save the Jews in the city of Susa from being killed. "Who knows," said Mordecai (her father), "Perhaps you have come to royal dignity for just such a time as this" (Esther 4:14). Who knows? Maybe the pilgrims who return to difficult churches will be used by God to renew them.

In more usual situations, pilgrims may find help in these suggestions from Bishop James Lloyd Knox[9] to "those who go through Emmaus and return to their congregations":

1. When you go back home don't be "holier than thou."
2. Get fully involved in the work of the church to use your experience at Emmaus.
3. Never let Emmaus and reunion groups become small, elite, superficially pious cliques.
4. Love everyone genuinely as a brother, sister, father, mother, son, or daughter.
5. Never be defensive about yourself, the church, or Emmaus.

Bishop Knox has offered sound advice that will go far toward enlivening local churches.

Leaven to Build Up the Church

Stephen D. Bryant, in *What Is Emmaus?*, uses the biblical image of leaven in the loaf to show the effect of Emmaus on the local church "Emmaus has a leavening effect in congregations. The leavening effect does not depend on congregation-wide participation but on the impact of a few lively, committed persons in the total chemistry of the church."[10] It is amazing what a little leaven will do in a loaf of bread. Yeast is small, but powerful beyond expectation. The Holy Spirit's influence in all of life is like leaven. As we return from Emmaus, we may be lively witnesses who are intentional about being disciples of Jesus Christ. We should see ourselves as leaven in local congregations, building up the church little by little and relying on the power of God to bring results. A realistic acceptance of the way things are; a fervent hope for the way things can be; and an honest effort to do all we can, while looking to God for results, is faith and wisdom at work.

A character in Robertson Davies' novel *The Cunning Man* said, "You must find a church that suits you, that you can stand and that can stand you, and stick with it."[11] Whether or not the Walk to Emmaus contributes to the renewal of congregations will be determined by Emmaus pilgrims and their commitment to local communities of faith. God calls us to "obedience over a long period of time and in a single direction." To be obedient, we "stick with it." We stay in the church for the long haul, relying on the power of God for renewal.

Don't Join the C. I. A.
(Cliques Illustrate Arrogance)

here is nothing secret about the Walk to Emmaus. Healthy spirituality is based on openness to God, ourselves, and one another. Jesus declared, "You will know the truth, and the truth will make you free" (John 8:32). He also pointed out the futility of trying to keep secrets: "Whatever you have said in the dark will be heard in the light, and what you have whispered behind closed doors will be proclaimed from the housetops" (Luke 12:3).

There is nothing secret about the Walk to Emmaus. But because of misperceptions and the actions of a few, the Walk has been charged with secrecy and elitism.

The Walk to Emmaus was created as a means of spiritual renewal for church members, who would then become influential in bringing renewal to their congregations and in making the world more Christian. Emmaus has been successful, beyond the wildest dreams of its founders. Emmaus has grown to include more than half a million pilgrims around the world.

What Does a Sponsor Do?
The Walk to Emmaus has a different way of recruiting participants than is customary in most church programs. People who have been on the Walk invite other people to attend and become their sponsors. Sponsors determine who, among the active members of a church, would be interested in attending a Walk, would benefit from it, and would extend those benefits to the congregation.

The sponsor's initial role is to explain to a potential pilgrim the purpose and format of the Walk so that he or she can make an informed decision about attending. The sponsor supports the pilgrim before the Walk and afterwards as the pilgrim integrates the Walk to Emmaus into his or her life. The sponsor helps to involve the pilgrim in a fourth day reunion group, takes him or her to a community reunion gathering, and guides him or her in the process of returning to the congregation. The Walk to Emmaus is an intense experience, and the pilgrim makes a commitment to be fully involved in the experience; the sponsor is expected to help with the pilgrim's concerns at home, such as child care or church responsibilities. In some communities, the sponsor also pays the pilgrim's expenses.

Sponsorship is perhaps the major reason for the Walk's success. It has done more than anything else to create informed participation. Pilgrims know what they are doing, and pastors and denominational leaders can support the Walk with confidence. Because of their sponsors, pilgrims are able to sustain discipleship after the weekend. However, sponsorship has also been mistakenly interpreted as exclusive and secretive. Some sponsors have contributed to the false impression by performing their responsibilities in a secretive fashion.

Anyone Can Attend

People who return from Emmaus should do everything they can to interpret the Walk openly. Emmaus is not elitist; anyone can attend. Sometimes individuals hear about the Walk to Emmaus and want to go. They initiate the process by asking "How can we go?" or "How do we find a sponsor?" Every effort should be made to find appropriate sponsors. Ideally, friends, relatives, or people from their congregation would be willing to sponsor them on an upcoming weekend. Otherwise, the local board of directors might ask pilgrims from another congregation to consider sponsoring them. It is common for people from one congregation to sponsor members of another church in order to introduce them to the Walk to Emmaus.

A young woman was staying for a period of time with a family from her church. Members of the family were active in their local congregation and in the Emmaus community. She kept hearing the words *Emmaus* and *Walk* and wondered what they could be talking about. Was it a secret society? a cult? When her host was asked to work on a team for a Walk, she finally asked, "What is this Walk to Emmaus anyway?" Her hosts gladly told her about the Walk. They gave her a copy of the booklet *What Is Emmaus?* and she read it eagerly. Later she told her host that she would like to go on a Walk to Emmaus. She was sponsored at the next possible weekend and continued to be active in her church and in the Emmaus community.

The same scene has been acted out in countless places, with

similar results. Unfortunately, there have also been situations in which people were given the impression that they had to "be somebody" or "know somebody" to participate. This is not true. We should make every effort to be open about the Walk to Emmaus.

Surprise!

Sometimes sponsors withhold information about the weekend so that they don't spoil any of the surprises. This is a ticklish problem. If we know too much about an upcoming event, we may develop preconceived notions and expectations that keep us from experiencing it fully. On the other hand, every Walk is unique because of the community of people who attend. The Walk to Emmaus is a definite program; and the participants need to know what they will be hearing and doing. They need to know that there are fifteen talks delivered by lay and clergy speakers, which constitute a short course on Christianity. If they want to know the titles of the talks and the gist of their content, they should be told. They need to know that communion will be served each day. If they want to know how it will be served, they should be told. People in the Emmaus community should listen to individual's concerns and openly offer information about the Walk. Emmaus is a little like Christmas: Some people want to know what they are getting. Others want to be surprised. Some people need to know what they're getting into in order to feel comfortable about Emmaus. Each person's need for information should be respected.

I have a friend who was abused as a child. The word *surprise* did not have a positive connotation for her. When I became her sponsor for a Walk, I could not say, "The Walk to Emmaus has some wonderful surprises; trust me." Instead, we went through the Walk schedule and I answered questions truthfully. She had a wonderful time.

A friend of mine told me that she had sponsored a person for the Walk and had told her everything she could about the experience. She took the weekend schedule and went through it step by step. She answered every question and didn't hedge on the answers. Still, the Walk was brand new for her when it happened. My friend said, "Everyone's experience is different and depends on where they are in their relationship to God. Emmaus may be a personal introduction to Christian faith or a renewal or a completely new track. They are all valid experiences."

I believe that some people enjoy the power of having information others don't have. They play "I know something you don't know" regarding the Walk to Emmaus. When prospective pilgrims want more information, they say, "Trust me. You'll love it." They stop talking about Emmaus when someone approaches who has not gone on a Walk. Worse yet, when a church member asks about the Walk, they hem and haw and evade the question. They come across like a spy: "I could tell you; but if I did, I'd have to kill you." Need I say that this kind of behavior works against everything we believe about the faith and fellowship of the church? I repeat: There is nothing secret about Emmaus.

Listen; Be Open

My advice is to listen to people. Whether they are participants in the Emmaus community, pilgrims on the next weekend Walk, or members of a congregation in which only some members have chosen to participate, let them set the agenda and ask for the information they need so that they will be comfortable with the Walk to Emmaus. We do not have to be evasive or apologetic or clandestine. We need to be open and honest and tell as much as others want to know about the Walk.

It is important for us to do everything we can to keep Emmaus from appearing cliquish. We should use common sense and courtesy and remember what it feels like to be excluded. The Bible tells about God's expansive hospitality and humanity's reluctance to accept it or to offer it to others. Pilgrims on the Walk to Emmaus should have picked up on the inclusive spirit of acceptance and courtesy that is part of Christian discipleship.

Beware Emmaus Cliques

We need to bend over backwards to avoid cliques in our congregations. Many congregations present Emmaus as an open community within the community of faith, not unlike a Sunday school class or a women's ministry circle or mission group. In these churches, fourth day reunion groups include a mix of people who have and have not participated in the Walk. Every reunion is an open invitation to everyone who wants to attend. Many good people have been sponsored because they first caught the spirit of Emmaus during a small group discussion or a pot luck supper at the church. As spiritual director for my Emmaus community, I once received a phone call asking if a pastor who had not attended the Walk to Emmaus could serve communion at a monthly reunion meeting. I replied that I thought his serving communion would be a wonderful idea and quite in line with both Emmaus and local church polity.

When Emmaus pilgrims hug one another but not other people, they make the Emmaus community appear cliquish. People who have shared intense experiences feel close to one another. But when the people of a congregation observe pilgrims hugging one another and shaking hands with everybody else, they wonder—and rightly so. If we are going to hug anybody, we should be ready and willing to hug everybody. (We should, of course, remember that hugging is not always welcome. 1 Corinthians 16:20 encourages the faithful to "greet one another with a holy kiss." The modern equivalent may be a Christian embrace, but it is up to individuals to communicate their feelings about hugging.)

The integrity of our experience during the Walk to Emmaus will be determined in large part by how we relate to people in our churches, both pilgrims and people who have not participated in Emmaus. I believe the Bible would advise us to walk wisely toward others. Wisdom means avoiding anything that could possibly paint Emmaus with the colors of cliquishness or secrecy. There is nothing secret about Emmaus.

Agape Unplugged

✛

O n my Walk to Emmaus, I experienced the overwhelming feeling of being loved. I couldn't believe that the team members would knock themselves out for my sake the way they did on that weekend. The decorations were delightful. The food was delicious. The speakers, lay and clergy, had taken the time to prepare their presentations. I remember being told that these and many other examples of genuine caring were acts of agape and that the entire Walk to Emmaus was an offering of agape to us.

Agape is the New Testament word for God's love expressed to, through, and by God's people. It is not erotic love or filial love or even altruistic love; agape is unconditional love expressed in specific ways for the benefit of the people who are loved. The Bible defines agape by showing us God's love expressed in Jesus' healing, teaching, and eating with sinners, as well as his dying and rising for them. It was also expressed in the life of the early church.

Love makes the Walk to Emmaus and any ministry of the church a powerful experience of salvation and redemption. When the church lives in the spirit of agape, the risen Christ is present and the gospel is proclaimed and experienced. The goal of the Walk to Emmaus is to show God's love to everyone involved. Every action and event in the seventy-two hours is designed to express the truth that we are loved. Emmaus is not perfect; but by intention and design, it is an expression of God's love.

The Bible talks about a church that turned "the world upside down" with love (Acts 17:6). Over the centuries, the church has changed. Most congregations have moved from being motivated by love to being motivated by duty or responsibility. The church has become like the church in Garrison Keillor's fictional Lake Woebegon: "Our Lady of Perpetual Responsibility."[12]

Emmaus has succeeded in renewing disciples and in sending them back to their local churches to be agents of renewal because it has provided them with a fresh awareness of how much God loves them. A pilgrim I know said, "I believe the essence of agape love is encountered on the Walks. There's this urge to share in how much Jesus really does love us. The scales of cynicism fall away. The compelling urge is to give Christ's love to another person."

Taking God's Love Home

The urge to share the love of God is given by God and makes acts of agape possible on the Walk to Emmaus; it also allows pilgrims to return to their congregations to help renew them in love. Robert Wood and Marie Livingston Roy state in their booklet, *Day Four: The Pilgrim's Continuing Journey*, "It is important to understand that agape is not limited to the Emmaus weekend, or even to the Emmaus community as a whole. Offering acts of agape—sacrificial love—on behalf of others in order that they may move closer to accepting God's love for them is a significant part of the continuing life in grace."[13]

Pilgrims should return from one expression of agape to another. Just as God has provided the Walk to Emmaus as an act of agape for those who participate in it, God has provided local congregations as acts of agape for the continued discipline and mission of God's people. Granted, implementing agape is easier to do in a seventy-two hour weekend than it is for the lifetime of a congregation. It is also easier with a few dozen people in a cloistered setting than it is with a few hundred people in a complex world. However, making people aware of agape in their lives and ministries may be the most important gift that Emmaus pilgrims take home to their communities of faith.

The goal of returning pilgrims should be to listen for the guidance of the Holy Spirit and to find ways to raise the intensity of love in their communities. Pilgrims do not return with new knowledge or skills, a manifesto for change, or easy solutions for all the church's problems. They return with empty hands; but with hearts filled with the love of God.

Practical Love

What would happen if love were the goal of every event in your church? What would change if people prayed for each program and then offered it to the church or community for the glory of God? What if the church's agenda were based on loving as Jesus loves? What if the chairperson of the board of trustees began by saying, "Our job is to use and care for our facility so that people feel the love of Christ when they are here." What would change if all the committees of the congregation sought to love God's people, rather than to do God's chores?

The goal of Emmaus is not to recreate the Walk in the local church or to recruit people for the weekend retreat. The goal is to return the spirit of agape, which is also the spirit of Emmaus, to the local church. As pilgrims return from Emmaus, they need to ask themselves questions such as these: How can I help my congregation be intensely loving? How can I help my congregation think of ministry as an act of agape?

Jesus said, "Just as I have loved you, you also should love one another. By this everyone will know that you are my disciples, if you have love for one another" (John 13:34-35). Returning to the congregation is above all a matter of returning with a greater awareness of and reliance on God's love.

In the excitement of the Walk to Emmaus, we sometimes forget that the purpose of the event is to develop Christian disciples who will renew local churches. How do pilgrims bring agape to their congregations? To be agents of renewal, they must make God's love tangible.

I've made a list of twenty ways to renew local churches. What would you add to the list? What is God calling you to do?

20 Ways to Renew the Church

1. Ask your pastor how you can be in ministry. (Bring smelling salts!)
2. Be the friendliest person at a church event.
3. Teach a Sunday school class.
4. Start a prayer group.
5. Sponsor a congregational leader for the next Walk to Emmaus.
6. Begin a Bible study group.
7. Help with the youth group; introduce them to Chrysalis.
8. Sponsor the pastor and his or her spouse a Walk.
9. Help the church secretary with the newsletter or other duties.
10. Write about the Walk to Emmaus for the church newsletter.

11. Visit the homebound for prayer and fellowship.
12. Visit people in the hospital.
13. Join the women's or men's group in the church. (If your church doesn't have a group, could you start one?)
14. Be a friendly usher at worship.
15. Volunteer to serve on the worship, mission, or evangelism committee or in another area of ministry that interests you.
16. Help with the church library.
17. Serve on the board of trustees; open the church building to the community.
18. Tithe.
19. Send agape to church members in crisis.
20. Start a program to feed the hungry or to shelter the homeless.

Remember: the real fourth day of the Walk to Emmaus involves the renewal of your church.

On Being in Your Pastor's Corner

(Rather Than Cornering Your Pastor)

✠

*A*n overzealous pilgrim cornered the new pastor, "I just want to know one thing: Are you Emmaus or not?" A district superintendent reported that before she was welcomed into some of the congregations in her district or asked about her vision for ministry, she was asked about her commitment to the Walk to Emmaus. Many pastors are cornered by people who desperately want to sponsor them on a Walk to Emmaus and will not take no for an answer. Such enthusiasm, though well intended, is not helpful.

What is a better approach to take? Pastors deserve the good will, confidence, and respect of their parishioners. They are spiritual leaders of their congregations and have been called by God. No matter what our intentions, when we tell other people that they *must* do something (especially when we point out that it is for their own good), their defenses are justifiably raised. Our pastors' participation in Emmaus and their opinions about Emmaus are secondary to our relationship with them, which should be based on mutual love and respect in Christ Jesus. Unless pastors know that we love and respect them, we have no business talking with them about the Walk to Emmaus. Our relationship with them is more precious and should be resolved first.

Sponsorship Is Discernment

Not everyone should participate in the Walk to Emmaus. God calls pilgrims, and sponsors should carefully consider whether it is God's will for a person to receive the gift of Emmaus at a particular time in his or her life. Sometimes, through prayer and conversation, a sponsor and a prospective pilgrim decide that attending the Walk is not an act of faith at that time. A decision not to attend the Walk is good reason to praise God for guidance. Sponsorship is not recruitment, but discernment. Discerning God's will is necessary even when the pilgrim is a pastor. Some clergy, like some laity, will choose not to participate in the Walk to Emmaus. A pastor's feelings about the Emmaus movement should have no bearing whatsoever on our love, respect, and support. Relationships based on love are part of our faithful response to Christ.

Our tendency is to get defensive when people oppose Emmaus or choose not to participate. After all, Emmaus is a program we love and believe in. God has blessed us with Emmaus as a model of Christian community that has touched hundreds of thousands of people and changed their hearts and lives. In the spirit of agape, we offer pastors and church members the opportunity to experience the Walk to Emmaus. We offer it with wisdom, careful consideration, and humility.

Often those who are initially cool to Emmaus later warm up to it. I went on my first Walk reluctantly. I was not happy about giving up seventy-two hours of my life to people I didn't know well so that I could engage in activities I didn't have enough information about. (My sponsor said, "Just trust me.") I had a wonderful, but difficult, time. My struggles with deeper dimensions of discipleship served as a counterpoint for the praise and fellowship that was part of the Walk. It took time for me to work through the weekend and to become an Emmaus supporter. Since then I have served on over a dozen Walks and have worked with Chrysalis. I have served on the board of directors for two Emmaus communities and on the International Steering Committee of the Walk to Emmaus. So there is hope, even for reluctant pilgrims!

Respect the Ministry of the Church

It is important to communicate that we value our pastors and their ministry. Pastors get so close to what they do for the Lord that there is often little space between their ministry and their identity. If we insist that our pastors participate in Emmaus, they may feel that we are diminishing their ministry.

Charles was the pastor of an inner-city church. When the subject of the Walk to Emmaus came up in his clergy support group, Charles went off like a gun, "One of my church members went on a Walk to Emmaus. He wasn't especially active in the church. Now he's involved in Emmaus. He asked me to go to a weekend. I told him no—and in no uncertain terms. Does he think the Holy Spirit is at a weekend retreat and not in the church every Sunday morning?" Charles was committed to ministry in a struggling congregation in a difficult location. He would have appreciated a pilgrim's offer to work beside him in the church. The Emmaus pilgrim erred by mistakenly assuming that the Holy Spirit's sole domain was the Walk to Emmaus. He should have shown his love and respect for Charles and the members of his local congregation by becoming involved in their ministry. Had the pilgrim returned from the Walk ready to work for renewal in his congregation, he would have modeled true discipleship and better served the purposes of Emmaus. Pastors and churches will not care how much we think of the Walk to Emmaus until they know how much we care about them and their ministry.

Pastors need to know that the Walk to Emmaus is a partner in ministry with local congregations. It is not a cult, trying to lure Christians away from their churches. There is nothing secret about the Walk to Emmaus. Information about every aspect of Emmaus is available from The Upper Room and should be offered to pastors and church members who have questions.

The Quality of Discipleship

The ministry of the Walk to Emmaus needs the support of pastors and denominational leaders. Pilgrims are responsible for representing the spirit of Emmaus to their pastors and congregations. We demonstrate our renewed faith in the quality of our discipleship as we live and serve in the church. Every Emmaus community is responsible for presenting the Walk as a way of renewing disciples and bringing new life to the local church. The Walk to Emmaus, local congregations, and denominations are "holy partners in a heavenly calling" (Hebrews 3:1).

Renewal and Inspiration

Emmaus is like an oasis; clergy and laity who have worked long and hard in the church need a time of inspiration and renewal. We may want to offer Emmaus as one way of being renewed, but not as the only way. We may want to talk with our pastors about the content of the Walk, a short course in Christianity similar to an adult confirmation retreat. We should show our pastors that pilgrims return from Emmaus with a new or renewed appreciation of the sacraments of the church and renewed faith in Christ as Lord and Savior. That's what pilgrims should do.

Is there something we shouldn't do? Yes. We shouldn't nag! Jesus said that the Holy Spirit is like the wind. "The wind blows where it chooses, and you hear the sound of it, but you do not know where it comes from or where it goes" (John 3:8). The Walk to Emmaus has been blessed by the Holy Spirit and has brought renewed spirituality to the church. As pilgrims to Emmaus, we let our pastors and congregations know of Emmaus's worth by the worthiness of our lives and by our commitment to and appreciation of local ministries.

My Cause Is Bigger
Than Your Cause

(God's Cause Is Bigger Than Both)

nyone who has attended a meeting of the administrative board or session of a local church or has sat through a denominational meeting knows the quandary of modern Christianity: Christians can't seem to agree. And disagreements can make church life pretty disagreeable. In *The City of God*, Saint Augustine pointed out that we are citizens of two cities, one on earth and one in heaven. We are part of the body of Christ and part of the body politic.

Church politics can get ugly. On the surface, Christianity seems so easy: "This is the message you have heard from the beginning, that we should love one another" (1 John 3:11). But how do we love one another when, in our humble opinion, others don't know what they're talking about? When people in the church have opposing points of view and understand the will of God differently, the church tends to lose its sense of Christian love.

Everybody Has an Opinion

We are victims of progress. In church and community, we are expected to witness persuasively and to speak and vote for or against more issues than our ancestors knew existed. At one time, an authority would have made decisions for us. Now we have the right to decide, and the number of people who make decisions increases all the time. At one time, only the clergy had a voice or a vote in the church; and the clergy were white men. We thank God that now all people— women, men, persons of color, persons of various ethnic origins— exercise their right to participate in the church. Increased diversity has made life in the church better, but more complicated.

We all want the support of our congregations. We all hope that other church members will take our side on political and social issues.

So the church is apt to take on the character of a shooting gallery, as all kinds of issues and concerns are raised for discussion.

A Community United in Christ

As important as it is for the church to take a stand on a broad range of social issues, it is more important for the church to stay focused on proclaiming the glorious good news of Jesus Christ and offering people access to God through a loving community. The church should find a way to struggle with political and social issues while transcending partisanship and maintaining a community defined by the love of Christ. We can get so busy with secondary issues that we lose sight of our primary mission: offering Christ to the world by being the church.

When the church loses its sense of community, it may lose its best witness to the world, the witness of a people who have found ways to disagree in love. When the church resembles a shooting gallery, people get caught in the crossfire; and friendly fire is just as deadly as enemy fire. Christians' fighting over issues is a testimony to sinfulness. Coercion, manipulation, and power politics weakens the church and its witness. When Christians prayerfully and humbly struggle with issues, they testify to the grace of God. Christian witness means carefully searching the Scriptures, collectively discerning the will of the Holy Spirit, and seeking consensus.

Given the complex nature of our lives and the increasingly strident nature of modern politics, it is little wonder that political partisanship has occasionally come to the forefront in the Walk to Emmaus. People have digressed from talk outlines to harangue the pilgrims about any number of contemporary issues. The board of directors of Emmaus communities has had to deal with zealots who wanted to use Emmaus as a power base from which to launch a crusade or reform. But God has not given us the Walk to Emmaus as a political forum. The Walk to Emmaus is a cooperative, ecumenical experience that brings together a diversity of people who have pledged to honor one another in Christian love. When people dishonor the pledge and change the agenda from living in Christ to expressing opinions on political or social issues, they undercut the love and good will that make the Walk to Emmaus possible.

Let's face it. Christians do not always agree; they argue about many controversial matters. The early church struggled over whether to eat meat offered to idols and whether to accept Gentiles into Christian fellowship. Over time, the people of God have differed on issues of war and peace, slavery, the use of alcohol and tobacco, wealth and poverty, abortion, violence, economics, sexuality. If our stance on any issue becomes a litmus test for orthodoxy, fellowship, or mission, we have misunderstand the nature of the Christian community and make it impossible to carry on the work of Christ together. Our unity in Christ does not depend on political uniformity.

Emmaus as a Political Community

I am not asking the church to be apolitical. I am asking Christians to bring to political discussions wisdom and humility. I am also asking that people refrain from political discussion on the Walk to Emmaus. We don't have to solve all the world's problems on a weekend Walk or through the Emmaus community. The fact is that if we offer the Walk as it is designed, remain faithful to the content of the talks, worship and pray together in Christian community, we are doing a radically political thing. Perhaps the best witness we can offer our polarized world is a view of community based on love and respect, in which people struggle prayerfully to include everyone in the community of faith. At Emmaus and in the congregations we return to, we give people a glimpse of the kind of community God wants for the whole world.

Jesus: The Way, The Truth, The Life

We should be humble and courteous with one another, giving one another freedom of thought and expression. Jesus said, "In everything do to other as you would have them do to you" (Matthew 7:12). We would do well to listen to him.

In their book *Of Course You're Angry: A Guide to Dealing with the Emotions of Chemical Dependence*, Rosellini and Worden encourage people to cut others some slack and to accept the fact that people will come down on different sides of every issue. They write, "There is a right way and a wrong way to do everything and the wrong way is to try to get everybody to do it the right way."[14] Christian discipleship is not converting others to our way of thinking or acting. After all, none of us has all the answers. We are all limited in our ability to perceive the truth and to know the way, but Christians do agree that Jesus is "the way, and the truth, and the life" (John 14:6). Instead of insisting on our own way, we should seek the Lord's way and focus on God's cause. Differences that seem impossible to resolve need not divide us, but they should humble us and move us toward the throne of grace to look to Christ for guidance on how to live together in a difficult world.

Pilgrims on the Walk to Emmaus are apt to have strong opinions and to take stands on complex issues; Emmaus encourages them to base their opinions on the gospel. However, the three-day Walk is not the time or the place to express personal biases; neither is the fourth day reunion. Emmaus does not provide each person with a soap box. The purpose of Emmaus is to involve people in a short course on Christianity. Emmaus cannot do everything for us or for the church. It cannot solve all our problems, heal all our wounds, or guide the world into a new tomorrow. That is God's job. It can only do what it is designed to do: to renew Christian disciples and, through them, to renew the church and the world. That agenda is enough and more than worthy of our best efforts.

Look to the Hills

During a debate over a controversial issue, a delegate to a denominational meeting referred to the Rocky Mountains as a fitting metaphor for an issue before the body. He said that the issue threatened to divide the denomination like water divides on the mountains, each raindrop seeking its own separate ocean. Is division inevitable? Must the body of Christ divide over issues? Perhaps we can see the mountains in another way, as we bring the issues we face to God's holy mountain, where with one heart and mind we lift our "eyes to the hills" and call on the Lord: "From where will my help come? My help comes from the Lord, who made heaven and earth" (Psalm 121). Maybe insurmountable mountains could show a humble church a better way.

On Not Being an Emmaus Groupie

✠

An anonymous wit summed up the gung-ho spirit fairly well: *Too much of a good thing is —just about right.* Even though we may want more and more, we realize that it is possible to overdo a good thing. Overdoing the Walk to Emmaus can do harm to pilgrims, their congregations, and the Emmaus movement itself.

Over the years, the Walk to Emmaus has had a profound effect on the lives of many people. Most have accepted the blessings of Emmaus and have assimilated them into their lives. With little or no problem, they have returned to their families and churches and have been better disciples because of the Emmaus experience. They have monitored their involvement with local Emmaus communities so that a healthy part of their time and energy has been invested in the work of Emmaus. They have wisely sponsored others for the Walk, worked on a team for a subsequent Walk, perhaps served on the local board of directors, and participated in reunion gatherings and small groups. This is the norm.

Others have gone overboard working for Emmaus. I call them Emmaus groupies. They resemble people who follow an entertainer and get so absorbed in his or her activities that they have no life of their own. Some people go on a weekend Walk and are so excited that they abandon their churches, families, and jobs to follow the appearances and activities of Emmaus. They feel that they have to serve in some capacity on every upcoming Walk. Within a year, they sponsor the chancel choir and the entire second shift at work. Fellow church members grumble that every other word they speak is *Emmaus.* Somebody needs to gently but firmly say, "Whoa."

When our lives get out of balance, we need to sort out our priorities. Other than The Upper Room staff, God hasn't called anyone to serve full time on the Walk to Emmaus. When pilgrims begin to approach full-time involvement in the Walk, they need to do some soul-searching. The aim of the Walk to Emmaus is to help the church make disciples. Disciples renewed by their involvement in Emmaus bring renewal to the church by investing themselves in the ministries of their congregations. The purpose of Emmaus is not to provide ongoing emotional thrills or spiritual highs. Involvement in Emmaus is a ministry of laity and clergy for the purpose of individual and church renewal. The people involved in Emmaus are going the second mile. The first mile of service should be traveled under the Lord's guidance in other areas of their lives.

How Many People? How Much Involvement?

A pyramid is a good image to describe the number of people involved in Emmaus activities after a weekend Walk. The pyramid serves solely as a symbol of the number of people involved and should in no way be understood as a hierarchy of authority.

▲ Fourth Day Reunion Groups

The most people are at the base of the pyramid. They are involved in fourth day reunion groups. While the weekend Walk to Emmaus is an event, continuing participation is primarily in small groups. Some people meet each week with between two and eight other Emmaus pilgrims, for prayer, support, and encouragement. Others prefer a more open approach and welcome anyone to join the group, regardless of their interest in or history with Emmaus. Regular participation in a fourth day small group is explained and encouraged on the Walk to Emmaus. The majority of Emmaus pilgrims are involved at this level.

Continued small group involvement in Emmaus is important to sustain spiritual growth and renewal. Long ago, John Wesley discovered the disciple's need for small group nurture: "I was more convinced than ever, that the preaching like an Apostle, without joining together those that are awakened, and training them up in the ways of God, is only begetting children for the murderer." He bemoaned the fact that in one area, twenty years of hard work had produced no societies and "the consequence is, that nine in ten of the once-awakened are now faster asleep than ever."[15] I wonder if the same could be said of Emmaus pilgrims who have not availed themselves of a fourth day group.

▲ Reunion Gatherings

At the next level of the pyramid are the reunion gatherings, spirited meetings in which pilgrims gather for worship, education, and community-building. Gatherings are scheduled on a regular basis by local Emmaus communities and offer a spiritual boost for pilgrims who attend. Gatherings are offered less frequently than the fourth day group, and fewer pilgrims regularly participate in them.

▲ Team Membership

The third level of the pyramid is team membership. At the request of the local team selection committee, people meet to prepare for and to implement weekend Walks. Working a Walk is an excellent way to grow as a disciple and to become more aware of the effort people put into a Walk to Emmaus. Being part of a team of servants for an Emmaus weekend is a blessing. Team members bring varying degrees of experience; some may work several times over a period of years and eventually assume responsibility for chairing a team or serving as a lay director of vice-director of a Walk. Each Emmaus community should establish a way of working so that people are well-trained in the process. Solid leadership by the team selection committee will prevent problems by guiding and counseling those who may have a tendency to go to extremes.

▲ Board of Directors

The next area of the pyramid is the Emmaus community board of directors. As with any Christian ministry, the work of Emmaus must be done in an orderly way. Each community makes a covenant with The Upper Room to present the Walk to Emmaus to its community. The Walk to Emmaus is a definite program. Who decides what is acceptable and unacceptable for a Walk to Emmaus? Each community's elected board of directors follows the instruction manuals provided by The Upper Room. The people who serve on the board of directors discern the will of God for their community in accordance with their covenant with The Upper Room. Some people with the gifts and calling of administration donate their time as members of the board of directors so that the Walk may continue to be offered to their community. A significantly smaller number of Emmaus pilgrims serve on a representative body at any one time.

▲ International Steering Committee

At the peak of the pyramid is the director of The Upper Room Walk to Emmaus program and the Walk to Emmaus international steering committee. An advisory steering committee has been established to provide information for the international director of the Walk to Emmaus. It is comprised of people from five regions of the United States and several other nations. I have had the privilege of serving on the international steering committee and consider it one of the great joys of my ministry in the church.

Whatever our involvement in Emmaus, we need to enter into it with prayer and faithfulness. The "Canon of the Emmaus Team" expresses the spirit of Emmaus participation.

Canon of the Emmaus Team [16]

I am a member of an Emmaus Team; therefore,
    I am only one part of a complete being!
I am an imperfect earthen vessel, and
I am here in a servant's role!
I will serve in humility and gratitude for the opportunity to be here,
    and will remember that the Holy Spirit calls for my love,
        patience, kindness,
        gentleness and self-control in all things!
I will pray for submission to the Spirit of this weekend
    and for strength and commitment to be God's person
    rather than my own person during these three days!
I will remember that I am here only as an instrument
    through which God can work to renew the church . . .

. . . I am only a servant; but God can use me more powerfully
    in this role than in any other that I might choose!
I am an imperfect earthen vessel,
    and am blessed to be here as a servant!
I am a member of an Emmaus Team;
In all things during this weekend
    I shall pray, "Not I, but Christ."

What is expressed in the "Canon of the Emmaus Team" is true for all participation in the Emmaus movement: "Not I, but Christ.

Whatever Happened
to Cleopas and His Friend?

✠

We all have old friends and acquaintances that we haven't seen in a while. *Whatever happened to old so and so?* we wonder momentarily, and then we move on with our lives. Occasionally, we may try to track down the person by phone or by mail. Detective agencies advertise that for a fee, they can find anybody on earth.

I wonder if anyone could find Cleopas and his friend. They were the two disciples who walked to Emmaus with Jesus (see Luke 24). The Upper Room chose Luke 24 as the biblical theme for the Walk to Emmaus, hoping that what happened to Cleopas and his friend would happen to participants in the program. And it has.

What happened to the two disillusioned disciples? They met the risen Christ. They were walking from Jerusalem to Emmaus into the setting sun. Was that why they didn't recognize Jesus when he "came near and went with them" (24:15)? More than likely, they weren't expecting Jesus to be anywhere but in a grave. They certainly didn't expect him to be walking with them to Emmaus.

The Walk to Emmaus is like the story of Cleopas and Jesus. Nobody expects to meet the risen Christ on a weekend Walk. After all, we've been to church retreats and meetings before; we know what to expect. Most of us are as surprised as Cleopas when, in the breaking of the bread, Christ is revealed to us. We may suddenly recognize Christ's presence at a communion service or a meal. What happened to Cleopas does happen to us at the Walk to Emmaus. We hear the word of God in talks by clergy and laity. We tell other people our doubts, our expectations, our dashed hopes. And along the way, our eyes are opened and we recognize him.

The Lord Has Risen and Has Appeared to Us

We don't know what happened to Cleopas and his companion. They were probably prominent leaders in the early church. Maybe when the first preachers told the story, they said, "If you don't believe me, just ask Cleopas. He'll tell you."

We don't know what will happen to us either. We don't know what the future holds for us or for the Walk to Emmaus. We hope that pilgrims will continue to bear witness to Christ by being disciples and working in their congregations for renewal. We believe that the local congregation is the primary focus of God's saving activity. The Walk to Emmaus will succeed or fail to the extent that participants return to their congregations and announce, "We have seen the Lord!"

We don't know what happened to Cleopas and his friend, but we do know what happened to Jesus. The disciples ran back to Jerusalem to tell the apostles about their amazing experience and were surprised to learn from the eleven, "The Lord has risen, indeed, and has appeared to Simon!" (24:34). No one doubted the authenticity of Cleopas' encounter with the risen Christ, but the Lord had appeared to the disciples as well. The story should remind us that the Walk to Emmaus is only one of many ways that Christ reveals his glory. Thank God for them all!

As I was rereading Luke 24, I came to a new insight. (Isn't that the way it is with the Bible?) I was looking for the ending of the passage. Most Bibles break the story after Cleopas' reunion with the other disciples, but the passage doesn't end there. While Cleopas and his friend were still there, Jesus appeared to them and taught them more about his role in God's plan of salvation. The text says, "Then he opened their minds to understand the scriptures" (24:45). Notice that open-mindedness is part of the story. I hope that Emmaus pilgrims will be open-minded disciples who have learned to set aside personal agendas so that they can experience the presence of Christ, become renewed disciples, and renew the church.

Luke 24 is a unit. The end of the story is the end of the gospel: "And they worshiped him, and returned to Jerusalem with great joy; and they were continually in the temple blessing God" (24:52). If that is not a return to the congregation, I don't know what is! The Walk to Emmaus, although valuable in its own right, is not complete until pilgrims have returned to their congregations with great joy in the Lord.

What happens to the Walk to Emmaus will depend in large part on the way we return to our congregations after the Walk and on how we continue our spiritual journeys as disciples of our Lord Jesus Christ.

End Notes

1 Friedrich Nietzsche, *Beyond Good and Evil: Prelude to a Philosophy of the Future*, translated by Walter Kaufmann; Vintage Books, 1966; page 101.

2 "I'll Go Where You Want Me to Go," *Hymns for the Family of God*; Paragon Associates, Inc., 1976; No. 502.

3 Dietrich Bonhoeffer, *The Cost of Discipleship*; SCM Press Ltd., Macmillan Paperbacks, 1970; page 60.

4 Eugene H. Peterson, *A Long Obedience in the Same Direction*; Intervarsity Press, 1980; page 17.

5 "God Moves in a Mysterious Way," *The Methodist Hymnal*, The Methodist Publishing House, 1964; No. 215.

6 Marjorie Thompson, *Soul Feast*; Westminster/John Knox, 1995; page 15.

7 John Wesley, *Hymns and Sacred Poems*, 1739; in *John Wesley's Works*, Volume XIV; Wesleyan-Methodist Book Room; page 321.

8 Steve Harper, *Devotional Life in the Wesleyan Tradition: A Workbook*; Upper Room Books, 1995; page 32.

9 Bishop James Lloyd Knox, personal correspondence to author.

10 Stephen D. Bryant, *What Is Emmaus?*; The Upper Room, 1995; page 32.

11 Robertson Davies, *The Cunning Man*; Viking Penguin, 1995; page 367.

[12] Garrison Keillor, *Lake Woebegon Days*; Penguin Books, 1985; page 2.

[13] Robert Wood and Marie Livingston Roy, *Day Four: The Pilgrim's Continuing Journey*; The Upper Room, 1986; page 35.

[14] Gayle Rosellini and Mark Worden, *Of Course You're Angry: A Guide to Dealing with the Emotions of Chemical Dependence*; Hazeldon Foundation, Center City, Minnesota, 1985; page 8.

[15] *The Journal of The Reverend John Wesley*, August 25, 1763; in *John Wesley's Works*, Volume III; Wesleyan-Methodist Book Room; page 144.

[16] *Team Manual: The Walk to Emmaus*, copyright © 1991 The Upper Room.

Resources

EMMAUS LIBRARY SERIES

What Is Emmaus? by Stephen D. Bryant ~ Answers frequently asked questions about Emmaus, the Emmaus community, and follow-up groups. #881

The Group Reunion by Stephen D. Bryant ~ For persons who have participated in the Walk to Emmaus, guidance on the purpose and practice of the group reunion. #884

The Board of Directors by Richard A. Gilmore ~ Responsibilities and duties of the board committees, possible committee assignments, and more. #883

Spiritual Directors by Kay Gray ~ Addresses the role of spiritual directors: qualifications; responsibilities before, during, and after the event. #886

Spiritual Growth through Team Experience by Joanne Bultemeier ~ A companion piece for the *Team Manual* and *Sustaining the Spirit*. Explains qualities of a team member, spiritual benefits of team membership, what happens at team meetings, and leadership development. #885

Coming Down from the Mountain: *Returning to Your Congregation* by Lawrence Martin ~ To help pilgrims make the transition back to their congregations, this booklet includes fun and informative chapters such as Long-Term Obedience in a Single Direction, Agape Unplugged, and On Not Being an Emmaus Groupie. #882

Walking Side by Side: *Devotions for Pilgrims* by Joanne Bultemeier and Cherie Jones ~ Forty-five meditations based on the fifteen talks given during The Walk offer a way to continue disciplines of prayer and meditation. #880

Sponsorship by Richard and Janine Gilmore ~ A guide through the process of sponsoring fellow pilgrims. Explores the range of possibilities in the role of the sponsor for the renewal of church leaders, Emmaus communities, and the church. #873

Music Directors by Sandy Stickney ~ Practical insights on topics ranging from ego to copyright requirements. Written with humor, directness, and a spirit of servanthood. #911

Additional resources for your journey toward piety, study, and action:

PIETY

Devotional Life in the Wesleyan Tradition by Steve Harper, #740

Dimensions of Prayer: *Cultivating a Relationship with God* by Douglas V. Steere, #971

A Guide to Prayer for Ministers and Other Servants, #460 (deluxe), #559 (paper)

A Guide to Prayer for All God's People by Norman Shawchuck and Rueben P. Job, #710

A Guide to Prayer for All Who Seek God by Norman Shawchuck and Rueben P. Job, #999 (deluxe), #1001 (paper)

Journeying Through the Days: *A Calendar & Journal for Personal Reflection*, annual

The Upper Room Disciplines: *A Book of Daily Devotions,* annual

Winter Grace: *Spirituality and Aging* by Kathleen Fischer, #850

STUDY

Discovering Community: *A Meditation on Community in Christ* by Stephen Doughty, #870

Journeymen: *A Spiritual Guide for Men (And Women Who Want to Understand Them)* by Kent Ira Groff, #862

Remember Who You Are: *Baptism, a Model for Christian Life* by William H. Willimon, #399

Remembering Your Story: *A Guide to Spiritual Autobiography* by Richard L. Morgan, #963

Shaped by the Word: *The Power of Scripture in Spiritual Formation* (rev. ed.) by M. Robert Mulholland Jr., #936

Sunday Dinner: *The Lord's Supper and the Christian Life* by William H. Willimon, #429

The Upper Room Spiritual Classics, Compiled and introduced by Keith Beasley-Topliffe: **Series 1** #832; **Series 2** #853; **Series 3** #905

The Workbook of Intercessory Prayer by Maxie Dunnam, #382

The Workbook of Living Prayer by Maxie Dunnam, #718

The Workbook on Becoming Alive in Christ by Maxie Dunnam, #542

The Workbook on Keeping Company with the Saints by Maxie Dunnam, #925

The Workbook on Lessons from the Saints by Maxie Dunnam, #965

The Workbook on the Beatitudes by Maxie Dunnam and Kimberly Dunnam Reisman, #9808

The Workbook on the Christian Walk by Maxie Dunnam, #640

The Workbook on the Seven Deadly Sins by Maxie Dunnam and Kimberly Dunnam Reisman, #714

The Workbook on Spiritual Disciplines by Maxie Dunnam, #479

The Workbook on the Ten Commandments by Maxie Dunnam and Kimberly Dunnam Reisman, #9875

The Workbook on Virtues & the Fruit of the Spirit by Maxie Dunnam and Kimberly Dunnam Reisman, #854

ACTION

And Not One Bird Stopped Singing: *Coping with Transition and Loss in Aging* by Doris Moreland Jones, #815

Prayer, Stress and Our Inner Wounds by Flora Slosson Wuellner, #501

Rediscovering Our Spiritual Gifts: *Building up the Body of Christ through the Gifts of the Spirit* by Charles V. Bryant, #633

Transforming Ventures. *A Spiritual Guide for Volunteers in Mission* by Jane Ives, #910

Yours Are the Hands of Christ by James C. Howell, #867

These Emmaus publications are available only from The Upper Room®:
> **Walk to Emmaus** (formerly Pilgrim's Guide #E1)
> **Lay Director's Manual** (#E4)
> **Spiritual Director's Manual** (#E27)
> **Lay Talk Outlines** (#E11)
> **Kitchen Manual** (#E15)
> **Day Four** (#9880)

TO ORDER CALL 1 (800) 972-0433.
Except as noted, resources are also available through your Cokesbury bookstore.